Lincoln's Use of the Bible

S. TREVENA JACKSON

Copyright ©2012 Big Fish Publishing

Chehalis, WA

ISBN-13: 978-0-9844692-7-7

When quiet in my house I sit,
Thy book be my companion still;
My joy thy sayings to repeat,
Talk o'er the records of thy will,
And search the oracles divine,
Till every heartfelt word be mine.
—Charles Wesley.

The Bible is a book of faith,
A book of doctrine,
And a book of religion,
Of especial revelation from God.
—Daniel Webster.

And weary seekers of the best,
We come back laden from our quest,
To find that all the sages said—
Is in the Book our mothers read.
—*Whittier.*

"The Bible is the king's best copy, the magistrate's best rule, the housewife's best guide, the servant's best directory, and the best companion of youth."

In a log cabin at Nolin's Creek, Hardin County, Kentucky, the boy breathed the first breath of life. Hope's anchor hung on a slender string, if we are to measure by the child's home surroundings. But his birthplace possessed a soul; for a home with a good book in it has a soul. This book was the Bible. It mastered his manners, molded his mind, made mighty his manhood, and gave to America the matchless man.

In the Bible he found the truth for the ills of men, the secret for the solution of life's perplexing problems, the boon for the best beaten path, the succor for the suffering, the calmest comforts for the dying, and the faithful friend when foes are near and other friends so far away.

We shall speak of what others have said concerning Lincoln's use of the Bible; what he himself said of it; the use he made of it; and the influence of the Scriptures on his life and literature.

In Herndon's Life of Lincoln the partner and President is portrayed as a foe rather than a friend of the Bible. This is seen to be erroneous by simply reading his speeches, for they are like the dewdrops on the blades of green in early fall, sparkling everywhere. It is hard to read a great speech of Lincoln's without seeing the influence of the Bible on his life, works, and style.

Sarah K. Bolton writes: "Mrs. Lincoln possessed but one book in the world, the Bible; and from this she taught her children daily. Abraham had been to school for two or three months, to such a school as the rude country afforded, and had learned to read. Of quick mind and retentive memory, he soon came to know the Bible well-nigh by heart, and to look upon his gentle teacher as the embodiment of all the good precepts in the book."

Lincoln's mother died after a lingering illness when he was ten years old. It is said that during her sickness he cared for her as tenderly as a girl, and that he often sat at her side and read the Bible to her for hours. Much of his later life and style was influenced by his early reading of the Bible.

L. E. Chittenden says: "Except the instructions of his mother, the Bible more powerfully controlled the intellectual development of the son than all other causes combined. He memorized many of its chapters and had them perfectly at his command. Early in his professional life he learned that the most useful of all books to the public speaker was the Bible. After 1857 he seldom made a speech which did not contain quotations from the Bible."

Alexander Williamson, who was engaged as tutor in the Lincoln family in Washington, said: "Mr.

Lincoln very frequently studied the Bible with the aid of Cruden's Concordance, which lay on his table." The Presbyterian pastor in Springfield, Rev. James Smith, states that Lincoln became a believer in the Bible and Jesus Christ as the Son of God. It is true that Mr. Smith placed before Lincoln the arguments for and against the divine authority of the Scriptures. He looked at it from a lawyer's viewpoint, and, at the conclusion, declared the argument in favor of divine authority and inspiration of the Bible unanswerable.

Mr. Arnold, in his Life of Lincoln, speaking of the Second Inaugural Address, said: "Since the days of Christ's Sermon on the Mount, where is the speech of emperor, king, or ruler which can compare with this? May we not without irreverence say that passages of this address are worthy of that holy book which he read daily, and from which, during his long days of trial, he had drawn inspiration and guidance? This paper in its solemn recognition of the justice of the Almighty God reminds us of the words of the old Hebrew prophets."

Bishop Simpson, in his funeral address, said: "Abraham Lincoln was a good man, a man of noble heart in every way. He read the Bible frequently; he loved it for its great truths; and he tried to be guided by its precepts. He believed in Christ as the Saviour of sinners, and I think he was sincere in trying to bring his life in harmony with the precepts of revealed religion. I doubt if any President has shown such trust in God, or in public document so frequently referred to divine aid."

In the year 1901 President Roosevelt delivered an address before the American Bible Society on "Reading the Bible," in which he said: "Lincoln, sad, patient, kindly Lincoln, who, after bearing upon his shoulders for four years a greater burden than that borne by any other man of the nineteenth century, laid down his life for the people whom, living, he had served so well, built up his entire reading upon his study of the Bible. He had mastered it absolutely, mastered it as later he mastered only one or two other books, notably Shakespeare, mastered it so that he became almost a man of one book who knew that book, and who instinctively put into practice what he had been taught therein; and he left his life as part of the crowning work of the century just closed."

Lincoln often spoke and wrote of the value of the Bible. To Joshua F. Speed, one of his most intimate friends, and at one time his roommate, he wrote: "I am profitably engaged in reading the Bible. Take all of this book upon reason that you can, and the balance on faith, and you will live and die a better man," Mrs. Speed gave Lincoln a Bible, and, after a visit to that home in 1841, he wrote to the daughter, Mary Speed, and at the close said: "Tell your mother I have not got her present (an Oxford Bible) with me, but I intend to read it regularly when I return home. I doubt not that it is really, as she says, the best cure for the blues, could one but take it according to truth."

On July 4, 1842, in writing to his friend Speed of the service he had been in bringing Joshua and Fanny, his sweetheart, together, he said: "I believe God made me one of the instruments of bringing you and Fanny together, which union I have no doubt he had foreordained. Whatever he designs he will do for me yet. 'Stand still and see the salvation of the Lord' is my text just now."

It is stated on good authority that after his election in 1860 he said to Judge Joseph Gillespie: "I have read on my knees the story of Gethsemane, where the Son of God prayed in vain that the cup of bitterness might pass from him. I am in the garden of Gethsemane now, and my cup is running over."

Lincoln's reply to a committee of colored people of Baltimore who presented him with a Bible, September 7, 1864, gives his opinion of the Bible: "In regard to this great book I have but to say: It is the best gift God has given to man. All the good Saviour gave to this world was communicated through this book. But for it we could not know right from wrong. All things most desirable for man's welfare here and hereafter are to be found portrayed in it. To you I return my most sincere thanks for the very elegant copy of the great Book of God which you present."

At Springfield he addressed the Bible Society and said: "It seems to me that nothing short of infinite wisdom could by any possibility have devised and given to man this excellent and perfect moral code. It is suited to men in all the conditions of life, and inculcates all the duties they owe to their Creator, to themselves, and to their fellow men."

In J. G. Holland's Life of Lincoln he gives us the conversation with Mr. Bateman: "Mr. Bateman, I have carefully read the Bible." Then he drew from his pocket a New Testament: "These men will know that I am for freedom in the territories, freedom everywhere as far as the Constitution and laws will permit, and my opponents are for slavery. They know this, yet, with this book in their hands, in the light of which human bondage cannot live a moment, they are going to vote against me. I know there is a God, and that he hates injustice and slavery. I see the storm coming, and I know that his hand is in it. If he has a place for me—and I think he has—I believe I am ready. I am nothing, but truth is everything. I know I am right, for Christ teaches it, and Christ is God."

In his Lyceum speech he speaks of the advantage of an education and being able to read the history of his own and other countries, by which we may appreciate the value of our free institutions, to say nothing of the advantages and satisfaction to be derived from all being able to read for themselves the Scriptures and other works both of a religious and moral nature. In this same speech he uses this language: "If destruction be our lot we must ourselves be its author and finisher." Then, speaking of the Revolution, he desired the history of it to "be read and recounted as long as the Bible shall be read."

The night before the President left Springfield for the White House a friend from Chicago sent him the American flag with these words: "Have not I commanded thee? Be strong and of a good courage; be not afraid, neither be thou dismayed: for the Lord thy God is with thee whithersoever thou goest. There shall not any man be able to stand before thee all the days of thy life: as I was with Moses, so I will be with thee."

It has been said by those who pride themselves on having no faith in the inspiration of the Scriptures that Lincoln held their views. But he addressed conventions and Sunday-schools, and the Bible was as often quoted by him as Blackstone. The addresses and letters of Lincoln are saturated with expressions from the Holy Scriptures. In his reply to Douglas he gave his speech great force by the words of Christ: "A house divided against itself cannot stand." In writing to Mr. W. Durley he uses scriptural terms: "By the fruit the tree is to be known. An evil tree cannot bring forth good fruit."

Ann Rutledge gave him a new view of the Bible and Shakespeare. Abraham Lincoln's is the language of the Bible. He never used the Bible in an irreverent way. In the Lincoln Museum, Washington, there is a copy of the Holy Scriptures. It is well worn, and shows the signs of good use. Inside the cover are these words in his own handwriting: "A. Lincoln, his own book."

He wrote a letter to Rev. J. M. Peck in 1848 asking him, "Is the precept, 'Whatsoever ye would that men should do to you, do ye even so to them,' obsolete, of no force, of no application?" In his description of Niagara he said: "It calls up the indefinite past when Christ suffered on the cross, when Moses led Israel through the Red Sea—nay, even when Adam first came from the hand of his Maker; then, as now, Niagara was roaring here."

In writing to John D. Johnston concerning his father's illness, he said: "I sincerely hope Father will recover his health, but, at all events, tell him to remember and call upon and confide in our great and good and merciful Maker. He notes the fall of the sparrow and numbers the hairs of our heads, and he will not forget the dying man who puts his trust in him."

Mr. William S. Speer wrote to Mr. Lincoln asking him to write a letter to give his definite views on the slavery question. Lincoln replied: "I have already done this many, many times, and it is in print and open to all who will read. Those who will not read or heed what I have already publicly said would not read or heed a repetition of it. 'If they hear not Moses and the prophets, neither will they be persuaded though one rose from the dead.'"

In a letter to Reverdy Johnson he wrote: "I am a patient man, always willing to forgive on the Christian terms of repentance, and also to give ample time for repentance." Lincoln wrote to General J. A. McClernand: "My belief is that the permanent estimate of what a general does in the field is fixed by the 'cloud of witnesses' who have been with him in the field."

Lincoln was ever bringing his knowledge of the Scriptures to the minds of men. When an aged citizen, John Phillips, had done him honor, he wrote him: "The example of such devotion to civic duties in one whose days have been already extended an average lifetime beyond the psalmist's limit cannot but be valuable and fruitful."

We find in his speeches and letters the Bible at his tongue's end. In his reply to Douglas at Alton he said: "He has warred upon them as Satan wars upon the Bible. The Bible says somewhere we are desperately selfish." And, writing to J. F. Speed, he writes of those who are so interested in slavery, and says: "If, like Haman, they should hang upon the gallows of their own building, I should not be among the mourners for their fate." Then again he says: "Let us judge not, that we be not judged," Then the words of the Christ: "Woe unto the world because of offenses! for it must needs be that offenses come; but woe to that man by whom the offense cometh!"

In his temperance speech in 1842 he sees the spirit of temperance like the conqueror in the Revelation going forth "conquering and to conquer," He sees the drunkard reclaimed, and, like the man in the gospel, "clothed and in his right mind"; then, describing the reclaimed, "out of their abundant hearts their tongues give utterance." Then he speaks of the unpardonable sin for the drunkard as unknown: "As in Christianity it is taught, 'while the lamp holds out to burn the vilest sinner may return.'" Then he refers to the Scriptures and says: "He ever seems to have gone forth like the Egyptian angel of death, commissioned to slay, if not the first, the fairest born of every family." Then he takes us over to the prophet: "Come from the four winds, O breath, and breathe upon these slain, that they may live."

He was very fond of a poem called "Adam and Eve's Wedding Song":

"When Adam was created
He dwelt in Eden's shade.
As Moses has recorded.
And soon a bride was made."

Some thought that Lincoln was its author, but he said: "I am not the author. I would give all I am worth, and go in debt, to be able to write so fine a piece." In speaking of the tariff he said: "In the early days of our race the Almighty said to the first of our race, 'In the sweat of thy face shalt thou eat bread.'"

In 1848, when President Polk sent a message to Congress stating that Mexico "had shed American blood upon American soil," Lincoln made a long speech against war with Mexico, and recalled the death of Abel thus: "That he [President Polk] is deeply conscious of being in the wrong; that he feels the blood of this war, like the blood of Abel, is crying to heaven against him."

In Lincoln's eulogy on Henry Clay he brings the Book of God before the people: "Pharaoh's country was cursed with plagues and his hosts were lost in the Red Sea for striving to retain a captive people who had already served them more than four hundred years. May this disaster never befall us!"

His knowledge of the Bible is clearly seen in his debate with Judge Douglas, for when the latter described man in the garden with evil or good to choose from Lincoln's reply was: "God did not place good and evil before man, telling him to take his choice. On the contrary, he did tell him there was one tree of the fruit of which he should not eat upon pain of certain death." Later Judge Douglas said that Lincoln had a proneness for quoting the Scriptures, and Lincoln replied in his Springfield address, July 17, 1858: "If I should do so now it occurs that he places himself somewhat upon the ground of the parable of the lost sheep which went astray upon the mountains, and when the owner of the hundred sheep found the one that was lost and threw it upon his shoulders, and came home rejoicing, it was said that there was more rejoicing over the one sheep that was lost and had been found than over the ninety and nine in the fold. The application is made by the Saviour in this parable thus: 'Verily I say unto you, there is more rejoicing in heaven over one sinner that repenteth than over ninety and nine just persons that need no repentance.' Repentance before forgiveness is a provision of the Christian system." In his fragments of a speech he claims "the revelation in the Bible, and his revelation the Bible."

Lincoln has before his mind the ideas of the early church when he says: "'Give to him that is needy' is a Christian rule of charity." In 1859 he gave a lecture on "Discoveries, Inventions, and Improvements," in which he gives a description of our first parents: "It was the destined work of Adam's race to develop by discoveries, inventions, and improvements, and the first invention of which we have any account is the fig-leaf apron. Speech was used by our first parents, and even by Adam before the creation of Eve."

At Cincinnati he speaks of "the loaves and fishes," and concludes his speech almost with Bible words: "The good old maxims of the Bible are applicable, and truly applicable, to human affairs; and in this as in other things we may say here that he who is not for us is against us; and he who gathereth not with us scattereth." He concludes his speech in Kansas in the same year with the same words.

When the people were anxious to hear and see him on his way to the White House he was desirous of keeping silence, and often quoted: "Solomon says there is a time to keep silence." At Philadelphia, in Independence Hall, he spoke: "All my political welfare has been in favor of the teachings that come from these sacred walls. May my right hand forget its cunning, and my tongue cleave to the roof of my mouth, if ever I prove false to these teachings."

When Lincoln proclaimed a national fast day he declared that all must be done in full conviction "that the fear of the Lord is the beginning of wisdom."

An old man had come to Lincoln for his son, who was to be shot, and said: "Mr. Lincoln, my wife sent me to you. We had three boys. They all joined your army. One of 'em has been killed, one's a-fighting now, and one of 'em, the youngest, has been tried for deserting, and he's going to be shot day after to-morrow. He never deserted. He's wild and may have drunk too much and wandered off, but he never deserted. 'Tain't in the blood. He's his mother's favorite, and if he's shot I know she'll die." General Butler was telegraphed to suspend the execution. The old man was afraid to go home with this message, thinking the President might give a different order to-morrow. Lincoln said to the old man: "Tell his mother that I said, 'If your son lives until they get further orders from me, when he does die people will say that old Methuselah was a baby compared to him.'"

It is said that the best result which the convention achieved at Cleveland in 1864, when it nominated Fremont for the presidency and John Cochrane for the vice-presidency, was that it called forth a bit of wit from the President. Some one remarked to him that, instead of the expected thousands, only about four hundred persons were present. He turned to the Bible which, say Nicolay and Hay, commonly lay on his desk, and read I Sam. 22. 2: "And every one that was in distress, and every one that was in debt, and every one that was in bitterness of soul, gathered themselves unto him; and he became a captain over them: and there were with him about four hundred men."

A primary and intermediate school was so located as to be separated by a fence from the rear of the White House grounds. The President often watched the children play. One morning the teacher gave them a lesson in neatness, and asked each boy to come to school next day with his shoes blacked. They all obeyed. One of them, John S., a poor one-armed lad, had used stove polish, the only kind his home afforded. The boys were merciless in their ridicule. The boy was only nine years old, the son of a dead soldier, his mother a washerwoman, with three other children to provide for. The President heard the boys jeering Johnny, and learned the facts about the boy.

The next day John S. came to school with a new suit and with new shoes, and told that the President had called at his home and took him to the store and bought two suits of clothes for him and clothes for his sisters, and sent coal and groceries to the house. In addition to this the lad brought to the teacher a scrap of paper containing a verse of Scripture, which Mr. Lincoln had requested to have written upon the blackboard:

"Inasmuch as ye have done it unto one of the least of these my brethren, ye have done it unto me."

Some weeks after the President visited the school, and the teacher directed his attention to the verse, which was still there. Mr. Lincoln read it; then, taking a crayon, said: "Boys, I have another quotation from the Bible, and I hope you will learn it and come to know its truth as I have known and felt it." Then below the other verse he wrote:

"It is more blessed to give than to receive.

A. LINCOLN."

The influence of the Bible on the life and literature of Lincoln was remarkable. It gave to this nation and the world a life of service, and in that service he placed the most delicate spirit of sincerity, sobriety, sympathy, and love. In literature he has given to us abiding beauty in its simplicity and strength of expression. Of his Gettysburg speech the London Quarterly Review said, substantially, that the oration surpassed every production of its class known in literature; that only the oration of Pericles over the victories of the Peloponnesian War could be compared to it, and that was put into his mouth by the historian Thucydides. Mr. Sumner said it was the most finished piece of oratory he had ever seen. Every word was appropriate. None could be omitted and none added and none changed.

Professor Albert S. Cook, teacher of English Language and Literature in Yale, in his book, The Bible and English Prose Style, seeking to show the influence of the Bible on the style of great writers, says: "But the matter is beyond dispute when we come to a piece of classic prose like Lincoln's Second Inaugural, which certainly owes nothing to the Romans of the Decadence." Then this sample of the Bible style is given: "'Neither party expected the magnitude or the duration which it has already attained. Neither anticipated that the cause of the conflict might cease with, or even before the conflict itself should cease. Each looked for an easier triumph, and a result less fundamental and astounding. Both read the same Bible and prayed to the same God, and each invoked his aid against the other. It may seem strange that any men should dare to ask a just God's assistance in wringing their bread from the sweat of other men's faces; but let us judge not, that we be not judged. The prayers of both could not be answered. That of neither has been fully. The Almighty has his own purposes!'

"At this point we may pause, for we need no further demonstration of the indebtedness of English prose style to the Bible, nor would it be easy to discover a better illustration of biblical qualities in modern guise exemplified in a passage of more interest to all the world. South recognized it as a mark of illiteracy to be fond of high-flown metaphors and allegories, attended and set off with scraps of Greek and Latin. If this be true, the American people so far escape the imputation as they have set their seal of approval on such writings as Lincoln's; and that they have had judgment and taste to do so is due, more than to any other cause, to their familiarity with the Bible."

The spirit life of the Bible was built into Lincoln's boyhood, expanded in his young manhood, ripened in his middle age, sustained him when sorrows seared his soul, and gave to him a grip upon God, man, freedom, and immortality. The influence of the Bible upon him gave him reverence for God and his will; for Christianity and its Christ; for the Holy Spirit and its help; for prayer and its power; for praise and its purpose; for the immortal impulse and its inspiration.

Truly might Henry Watterson ask: "Where did Shakespeare get his genius? Where did Mozart get his music? Whose hand smote the lyre of the Scottish plowman, and stayed the life of the German priest? God, God, and God alone, and surely as these were raised up by God, so was Abraham Lincoln."

www.ingramcontent.com/pod-product-compliance
Lightning Source LLC
Chambersburg PA
CBHW031440040426
42444CB00006B/900